INNER HEALING

A Spiritual Approach to Dealing With Conflict
and Healing From Hurt

By

Bishop Youssef

INNER HEALING: A Spiritual Approach to Dealing With Conflict and Healing from Hurt

By Bishop Youssef

Copyright © 2022 Coptic Orthodox Diocese of the Southern U.S.A.

All rights reserved.

Designed & Published by:
St. Mary & St. Moses Abbey Press
101 S Vista Dr, Sandia, TX 78383
stmabbeypress.com

All Scripture quotations in the footnotes of this book, unless otherwise indicated, are taken from the New King James Version® Copyright © 1982 by Thomas Nelson, Inc. Used by permission. All rights reserved.

Library of Congress Control Number: 2022944144

CONTENTS

Introduction 5

1 Non-Biblical Ways for Dealing With Hurt 6

2 Biblical Principles for Dealing With Hurt 13

3 Healing, Forgiveness, and Reconciliation. 27

INTRODUCTION

Throughout our lives, we inevitably face conflict with those around us—those we live with, those in the church community, those at work and those with whom we interact in our daily lives. As conflict arises, we have a choice regarding how to deal with it. Generally, there are two approaches to conflict resolution: a worldly approach, and a spiritual, biblically-based approach. The first usually centers on egotistical principles of physical self-protection; sadly, though, while that approach can temporarily seem satisfying, it eventually leads to negative results and loss of peace. The second approach—spiritual and biblically-based—leads to truly resolving conflict and to inner healing.

This book, based on lectures given by His Grace Bishop Youssef at the Institute of Counseling in Maadi, Cairo, addresses these approaches and the psychological nuances one experiences once the decision is made to approach the conflict worldly or spiritually.

CHAPTER

1

NON-BIBLICAL WAYS FOR DEALING WITH HURT

As long as people live together, they will inevitably encounter hurt from others. It is unavoidable!

It is impossible for any of us to say, "I have never hurt anyone's feelings, intentionally or unintentionally." It is also impossible for anyone to say, "I have never been hurt." Therefore, as long as we may hurt each other's feelings, and could be hurt by one another, we need to know how to react in a healthy way. With a non-biblical mindset, people tend to react in one of four self-protective approaches. None of these ways are aligned with the teachings of the Holy Bible.

First Approach: Responding to an Offense With an Offense

> He that takes vengeance will suffer vengeance from the Lord, and he will firmly establish his sins. Forgive your neighbor the wrong he has done and then your sins will be pardoned when you pray. (Sirach 28:1,2)

In this approach, when someone insults me, I insult him back. If someone disrespects me, I, in turn, do the same back, forgetting that this is an Old Testament law, which taught: "An eye for an eye, a tooth for a tooth" (Exodus 21:24). Many of us respond to an offense with another offense, and to a hurt with another hurt. This response might be overt or covert. The overt response is to repay an insult with an insult. In the covert response—which Psychology calls "passive-aggression"—I ignore the other person, or make fun of them. Also, if someone reproaches me, I say "I was only kidding." That is, I try to act in a calm yet irritating way. This is the passive-aggressive response to repay an insult.

Second Approach: Avoidance and Hostility

In this approach, one becomes hostile or avoids the offender. Many of us try to justify this response by saying, "I love and forgive this person, but he causes me to stumble; so it is best for me to stay away." However, the Holy Bible did not teach that if your brother sins against you, stay away from him; rather, it says, "If your brother sins against you, go and tell him his fault" (Matthew 18:15).

Many people say, "I do not like to confront because confrontation causes problems," but when our life is Bible-based, we realize that it is impossible for our Lord Jesus Christ to give us a commandment that would cause problems. If confrontation causes problems, then we must examine if the fault is in not knowing how to confront.

Third Approach: Gossip and Slander

In this approach, one vents their anger and irritation to others, getting revenge by slandering the offender.

Fourth Approach: Ignoring My Feelings

In this response, one pretends to have never been hurt. But similar to wounds that develop infection if left untreated, ignoring one's feelings can lead to psychological scars. The Holy Bible does not teach us to ignore our feelings, or it would not have said, "Be angry, and do not sin" (Ephesians 4:26). We need to express our feelings, but in the right way.

In summary, the four non-biblical responses of dealing with hurt are:

- Repaying an offense with an offense
- Becoming distant or hostile to the offender
- Gossiping about the offender
- Ignoring the offense as if it never occurred

Amazingly, there is a common thread along these four approaches: in each one, I am trying to protect myself. How? Let us take each approach and dig deeper.

When I insult whoever insults me, I am telling that person, "I am not letting this slide, so, don't you dare wrong me again, because I will stop you, will insult you, and will tear you apart." I am protecting myself.

In the second approach, when I am brief, I am hiding behind a shield to protect myself, trying to tell the other person, "You will not be able to reach me to hurt me again. I will not give you the chance to reach me and do it again, so I will be brief and stay away from you." I am protecting myself.

In the third approach, when I gossip about the offender with others, I am forming a group to take my side against, and gossip about, them. This way, I am sending a message saying, "If you hurt me again, I am not facing you alone, I have ten or fifteen people who know that you are a bad person." Again, it is a form of protecting myself.

In the fourth approach, when I ignore the offense, I am sending a message that says, "Do not think you can irritate me, upset me, or hurt me. I am above being hurt by you." I am sending a message that I am beyond being hurt. Unfortunately, this is not true, because we are all humans, we all get hurt, and no one is above being hurt.

Following the Commandments

Acting out of self-protection means I do not want to take the risk of carrying out the commandments. But we know there is discomfort in fulfilling any commandment when we are have not surrendered to the Lord. For example, when God tells us to "bring all the tithes" (Malachi 3:10), we have a nagging question: If I bring ten percent of my income, will the ninety percent suffice? Similarly, when our Lord said, "Turn the other cheek" (cf. Matthew 5:39), it is a serious challenge. Am I ready to take it or not? And when He said, "If your brother sins against you, go and tell him his fault" (Matthew 18:15), there is a challenge here too—the Lord Christ warned us that the other might not listen.

Am I ready to take this risk? When our Lord told Peter to come out of the boat, Peter took the risk. He could have sunk, but obeying the Lord's word, he came down and started to walk on water. As soon as Peter started to look to himself, he began to sink. These examples show that following the commandments involves risk or challenge, but if we have faith and surrender to God, the commandments will definitely protect us.

When one does not fulfill the commandments, but rather responds with one of the four non-biblical approaches, one is implicitly saying, "Lord, I am in charge here, stay away! Your commandments can hurt me, so I will not follow them. I will solve the problem in my own way." By trying to protect ourselves, we block the protection our Lord provides through His commandments. It is very dangerous to rely on self-protection instead of allowing God to protect us. This is why, we, as children of God, should not resort to any of these four worldly, non-biblical approaches.

CHAPTER 2

BIBLICAL PRINCIPLES FOR DEALING WITH HURT

The Holy Bible offers four principles for dealing with hurt and insult.

First Principle: Reconcile!

In the Sermon on the Mount, St. Matthew stresses the importance of reconciliation: "Therefore if you bring your gift to the altar, and there remember that your brother has something against you, leave your gift there before the altar, and go your way. First be reconciled to your brother, and then come and offer your gift" (Matthew 5:23–24).

One must put three lines under the word "first" in the Holy Bible. Why? Because the Church and the Holy Bible teach that worship takes priority over all other activities. Reconciliation with your brother is the only action that takes priority over worshipping God.

Why is reconciliation given priority, even over worshipping God? Because without reconciliation, our worship will be rejected! Pray for as long as you want to pray, read the Holy Bible as much as you want to read, attend as many Divine Liturgies as you want to attend, fast as long as you want to fast—but if you are not reconciled, your worship will be rejected. These are the words of the Holy Bible. We read in the Book of Malachi that some people were praying fervently, to the point of drenching the Lord's altar with tears and weeping (imagine someone praying to the point that his tears cover the altar), yet God did not heed their prayers: "And this is the second thing you do: you cover the altar of the Lord with tears, with weeping and crying; so He does not regard the offering anymore, nor receive it with goodwill from your hands" (Malachi 2:13). Even what you offer, to please God, to obtain His goodwill, He will not accept from your hand. "Yet you say, 'For what reason?'" (Malachi 2:14). People were confused, "Why God, am I praying to You with tears and weeping, and am presenting offerings to You, trying to please You, but You refuse. What is the reason?" "Because the Lord has been witness between you and the wife of your youth, with whom you have dealt treacherously; yet she is your companion and your wife by covenant" (Malachi 2:14). "Will you actually argue and quarrel with your wife, and come to pray, wanting Me to accept your prayer? No!"

One must realize that with regard to reconciliation, the phrase "dealt treacherously with your wife" also applies to your brother, your neighbor, your friend, and your enemy. "Go your way. First be reconciled to your brother. I cannot accept your sacrifice, your offering, your prayer, nor your worship, until you reconcile."

Lest someone protest that this is the Old Testament, let us be clear that the New Testament reiterates the same condition for acceptable worship. Saint Peter the Apostle gives stern advice: "Husbands, likewise, dwell with them with understanding, giving honor to the wife, as to the weaker vessel, and as being heirs together of the grace of life, that your prayers may not be hindered" (1 Peter 3:7). What does "that your prayers may not be hindered" mean? If you are upset with another person (refusing to reconcile) and you stand to pray, there will be a barrier preventing your prayers from reaching the Lord. This is why God said, "Go your way. First be reconciled to your brother," and then come to pray, because, had you prayed, your prayers would have been hindered from reaching God due to the conflict between you and the other.

The Spirit-inspired Church established the holy kiss during the Divine Liturgy. During the Prayer of Reconciliation (which is about reconciliation with God), the priest holds up a triangle-shaped veil, symbolizing the veil that separated us from God. At the end of the prayer, while the deacon is holding the cross opposite him, the priest lays down the veil, symbolizing the veil being torn asunder by the cross, and our subsequent reconciliation with God. However, the deacon chants an amazing response that has nothing to do with reconciliation with God, but rather reconciliation with each other. He says, "Greet one another with a holy kiss," as if the Church is telling us, "You cannot reconcile with God, unless you reconcile with your brother first." It is impossible for you to be at peace with God while you are in conflict with your brother. Go and be reconciled with your brother first, and then you may be able to reconcile with God.

But what happens if I am not reconciled with my brother and I take communion anyway? In the Prayer of Reconciliation in the Saint Basil Liturgy, the priest says: "And make us all worthy, our Master, to greet one another with a holy kiss, that without casting us into condemnation we may partake of Your immortal and heavenly gift." We are saying, "Lord, make us worthy to greet one another with a holy kiss." Why? "So that, when we partake of Your immortal heavenly gift (Your Body and Blood), we are not cast into judgment, or condemnation." The communion that God gives me for my salvation and the forgiveness of my sins, can be a cause of casting me into judgment and condemnation, if I partake while not reconciled with my brother!

Some people use trickery. If they are at odds with someone standing in the first row in church, they stand five rows back, so that when the deacon says to greet one another, they are too far to greet one another. However, you can deceive yourself and your father of confession, but it is impossible to deceive our Lord. When the deacon says "greet one another," that includes not only those in your same bench in church, but every person in your life, whether they are present at church or not; you should be able to greet that person with a holy kiss.

What is the definition of a holy kiss? In the Prayer of Reconciliation from the Saint Cyril Liturgy, we say: "Not with a vile sense that defies Your fear, nor with thoughts of guile filled with the wickedness of the traitor, for our conscience is not bent on wickedness, but rather by the eagerness of our souls and the rejoicing of our hearts, having the great and perfect sign of the love of Your only-begotten Son."

Therefore, we see that the Liturgy gives three conditions for the Holy kiss:

"Not with a vile sense." Often, worldly people use a kiss to express sinful desires; but spiritual people greet each other in purity.

"Nor with thoughts of guile filled with the wickedness of the traitor." Who is the traitor? Judas, because he said, "'Greetings, Rabbi!' and kissed Him" (Matthew 26:49). One should not greet a person saying, "How are you doing? I've missed you," while gossiping and stabbing this person in the back. This is not a holy kiss; this comes only from a person filled with the wickedness of the traitor. We must not behave like that. One might ask, "Must I greet this person in order to take communion?" And because the answer is an emphatic "yes," he goes through the motion of greeting the person, but with an impure heart. This is totally rejected.

"But rather by the eagerness of our souls and the rejoicing of our hearts." When you greet someone, you do so with longing and rejoicing. "How can I greet this person who hurt me with longing, desire, and rejoicing?" By "Having the great and perfect sign of the love of Your only-begotten Son," the sign of the cross, which the Lord Christ endured in order to reconcile us with Him. If I carry the cross in my life, rejoicing for the joy laid before me when I go to greet my brother, I will greet him with "eagerness of soul and rejoicing of heart."

This is why ordination of priests and deacons occur after the prayer of reconciliation, symbolic of their work in reconciliation: "We are ambassadors for Christ, as though God were pleading through us: we implore you on Christ's behalf, be reconciled to God" (2 Corinthians 5:20).

The Second Principle: Be Honest and Sincere

In Ephesians 4:25, Saint Paul says, "Therefore, putting away lying, let each one of you speak truth with his neighbor." If I come to ask if you are upset with me, and you answer, "No, nothing is wrong," but in your heart you are upset, then you are lying. If I ask you if something is wrong, you could answer, "Yes, actually something is bothering me." The verse continues, "For we are members of one another. Be angry, and do not sin." There is nothing wrong with expressing your anger, saying, "I am annoyed. I am upset," yet, expressing it without sinning.

St. Paul continues, "Do not let the sun go down on your wrath" (Ephesians 4:26). One needs to rectify relationships with others as quickly as possible. Why? Most of us have memorized the verse that says, "Do not let the sun go down on your wrath," but many might not remember the rest of the verse, which says: "Nor give place to the devil" (Ephesians 4:27). The rest of the verse is very important, because Saint Paul is saying that the longer the period of the quarrel, the more room you give to the devil. You are inviting him to sit with you. If you are upset with your brother for an hour, you have invited the devil to penetrate your relationship for an hour. If for a week, then you have invited the devil to join you for a week. If for a year, then you have given the devil a place to reside, you have given him residency. If for five years, then you have given him citizenship in your relationship. Whoever wants to keep the devil abiding in their relationships will not reconcile, but the one who wants to evict the devil will reconcile immediately. The devil sows discord; God is the King of Peace. The longer the dispute drags on, the more space there is for the devil.

The Third Principle: Maintain Peaceful Relations With All

Romans 12:18 states "If it is possible, as much as depends on you, live peaceably with all men." Unfortunately, many misinterpret this verse. Notice that the verse says "as much as depends on you," not "according to your ability." If you are upset with me, for me to reconcile with you, I have to act, and you have to act. If I act, but you do not act, then we will not be reconciled, although I thoroughly followed through with my part. Take for example our Lord. He was incarnate and was crucified to reconcile us to Himself. However, not all people are reconciled with God? Why? Because some people chose not to reconcile with God, although He did "as much as depended on Him." He did all that He could possibly do, and yet, some people are not reconciled with Him, because they did not do their part. Saint Paul says, "as much as depends on you, live peaceably with all men," meaning you need to put in 100 percent so that the only acceptable excuse before God for your division is that the other party refuses to reconcile. This is when you will be blameless. Here is where you can take communion and pray, and God will accept your prayers, because you have given 100 percent. You cannot excuse yourself saying, "This is all I can put in. My limit is 30 percent, my limit is 50 percent." No. Your duty is to do as much as depends on you. What was the Lord's duty to shed His blood on the cross? I have to go the extra mile; I need to be willing to shed my blood in order to live in peace. If I do all this, and the other party refuses, there is nothing more I can do. However, beware of being an opponent and judge simultaneously. Do not say, "I did everything I could. That is it! I will pray and take communion, although I am not reconciled with others." No, you cannot be an opponent and judge. The church is the one who judges if you have fulfilled your role, and the other is now to you "like a heathen and a tax collector" (Matthew 18:17). In this case, you will be permitted to take communion and your prayers and worship will be acceptable before God.

The Fourth Principle: Be the First to Extend the Olive Branch

The Bible is very clear on this: "Moreover, if your brother sins against you, go and tell him his fault between you and him alone. If he hears you, you have gained your brother. But if he will not hear, take with you one or two more, that 'by the mouth of two or three witnesses every word may be established.' And if he refuses to hear them, tell it to the church. But if he refuses even to hear the church, let him be to you like a heathen and a tax collector" (Matthew 18:15–17).

So the question here is whether to follow the Bible's commandment or follow the worldly norm that the one who is at fault should start the reconciliation process.

For example, in trying to reconcile a couple, you might say, "Come, let us talk to your wife." If the husband replies, "No! She offended me, so she must come to me"—that is a worldly response. But the Bible says clearly that you should go first to the person who sinned against you.

This previous illustration reveals a very important principle to keep in mind: children of the devil initiate problems, children of God initiate peace and reconciliation. John 3:10 states "The children of God and the children of the devil are manifest." So we must ask ourselves: to which group do we want to belong?

To further illustrate how a proper reconciliation process starts, imagine you are standing on a crowded bus, and a person steps on your foot (perhaps by accident). Who feels the pain? You! And what happens? You probably say, "Excuse me, you are stepping on my foot!

It hurts!" This clearly shows us that it can be natural for the person feeling pain to be the one who expresses it. Similarly, if I offend you, perhaps I have done it by accident and I am unaware, so it is helpful to come and tell me: "Pardon me, but this word hurt me, this word offended me." This is how we begin the process of reconciliation.

In summary, the four principles of reconciliation are:

- Act quickly; do not let the sun go down on an argument, so as not to give place to the devil.
- Give priority to reconciliation, even over worship.
- Give your full capacity and effort to the reconciliation process.
- Initiate the reconciliation process regardless of being the offender or the offended.

Let us follow God's example for reconciliation: when Adam and Eve broke the commandment, God's actions show these four principles in action.

First principle: God had reconciliation as a priority, otherwise, why would He have become incarnate and died on the cross? God had no need to reconcile with us. If the entire world ceases to exist and perishes, would that have affected God? No. However, because our Lord is the King of Peace, He initiated the reconciliation process with us.

Second principle: The sun did not set before God initiated the reconciliation process in the same day, as we read in Genesis 3:8: "In the cool of the day." When Adam sinned, he hid from the presence of God, but before the sun went down, God was looking for him: "The Lord God called to Adam and said to him, 'Where are you?'" (Genesis 3:9). Note that the reconciliation process takes time. Nevertheless, our Lord started on the same day that Adam sinned. He did not wait, being upset with him, or avoid him for a month or so and then begin to look for him. He looked for Adam on that very day, "in the cool of the day," before the sun went down.

Third principle: God gave more than 100 percent of His capacity and effort for reconciliation. He took flesh, and He gave His only begotten Son to be crucified.

Fourth principle: God initiated the reconciliation. Adam did not apologize, but rather he blamed Eve, and she in turn blamed the serpent. Nevertheless, our Lord promised them reconciliation: the Seed of the woman would crush the head of the serpent (cf. Genesis 3:15).

God showed us how to apply these four principles because "Greater love has no one than this, than to lay down one's life for his friends" (John 15:13). As children of God, we must follow His path in reconciling with others.

CHAPTER

3

HEALING, FORGIVENESS, AND RECONCILIATION

For successful application of the previous principles, we must make a clear distinction between three terms: healing, forgiveness, and reconciliation. What is the difference among these three words?

If I have an injury, this injury needs healing. Healing means I start feeling better and my feelings go back to normal. This is inner healing.

Forgiveness means I extinguish the entitlement to a debt that I hold against the other person; when someone offends me, I have a right to an apology, a debt owed to me.

When I forgive someone, I absolve this debt saying, "You are no longer indebted to me. I forgive you."

Reconciliation is restoring the relationship to its earlier state, or even improving it:

- Healing = Hurt feelings are restored to normal.
- Forgiveness = Forgoing a right I have over you, tearing up a debt.
- Reconciliation = Returning to my earlier relationship with you, or even better than before.

INNER HEALING

There are a few very important principles about healing.

First: The person who hurt you is unable to heal you, and cannot make you feel better. The only one who can cure your wounds is God, "the true Physician of our souls and our bodies" (Litany of the Sick). Our problem is that often we await the one who hurt us to be the one who makes us feel better again. This is illogical. To illustrate, if a car hit and injured me as I crossed the street, will I ask the person who hit me to cure my injuries? What if he is not a physician? My injury will only worsen. He is unable to treat me. If I am injured, I need to go to the hospital, to a physician, and seek treatment. Many of us seek inner healing from the one who caused the injury, but only the true Physician is able to heal.

Second: For inner healing to occur, two very important components are needed. One is forgiveness, and the other is reconciliation. Without these two, the inner healing process cannot be completed. Many people say, "Let me calm down first, recover a little, and then I will forgive and reconcile." This is exactly like someone saying, "Let me heal first, and then I will take the medicine." This does not work. This is the reason the Lord Jesus, while in the midst of His pain on the cross, did not say, "Give Me some time to calm down and then I will forgive," but rather said, "Father, forgive them, for they do not know what they do" (Luke 23:34). The same goes for Saint Stephen; in the midst of his pain, while being stoned, he said, "Lord, do not charge them with this sin" (Acts 7:60). Both Jesus and St. Stephen forgave the debt, because they knew that forgiveness and reconciliation are vital to the healing process. If someone hurt you, forgive them, go reconcile with them, and you will find that inner healing begins.

Third: In inner healing, as in medicine, some illnesses prolong the healing process. If a physical wound does not heal quickly, a physician might discover that the underlying reason is diabetes. Therefore, the diabetes needs to be controlled, and then the wound will heal. The same applies in spiritual life—some spiritual illnesses delay inner healing. To heal quickly, one needs to remedy these spiritual weaknesses—hatred, intolerance, disdain, vengeance, non-forgiveness, over-sensitivity, ego, pride—all these illnesses delay inner healing and need to be treated before healing can occur. As long as these illnesses exist, healing is suspended. In order for the hurt you are experiencing to heal, you need to treat these illnesses.

Fourth: Accept responsibility for your mistakes, so you can heal. If there is a disagreement between the two of you, it is likely that you have both made mistakes. If you say it is entirely the other person's fault, and you are completely innocent, then you will never heal. Often, in family disagreements, the husband claims that his wife is the culprit and he is innocent, and the wife likewise claims that her husband is the cause of all the problems. Saint James the Apostle teaches us this rule: "Confess your trespasses to one another, and pray for one another, that you may be healed" (James 5:16). This means I must come to confess to you that I have wronged you, that I did such and such, and that I take full responsibility for my mistakes. This will heal my pain. Trying to put all the blame on the other person, and claiming to be a saint, will never help me heal.

Four principles for inner healing:
- The person who caused the hurt is unable to heal; God is the true Physician.
- Forgiveness and reconciliation are two essential components for the healing process.
- Spiritual illnesses that hinder healing must be treated before healing can occur.
- Assume responsibility for your mistakes, and admit them before yourself, before God, before your father of confession, and before the person you offended, so you may be healed.

FORGIVENESS VERSUS RECONCILIATION

Forgiveness is extinguishing [tearing up] the debt; reconciliation is reinstating the relationship.

On the cross, our Lord forgave all sins for all people throughout time, but He did not reconcile with everyone, because some people refused to reconcile with Him. This is why we say that God forgave our sins and "restored our father Adam and his children to Paradise" (Divine Liturgy Fraction Prayer for the Resurrection). Restoring is reinstating the relationship to its prior state or better than before. Our Lord Jesus Christ restored our relationship with Him even beyond even its earlier condition.

Forgiveness depends solely on you; reconciliation depends on both parties.

You can forgive me of your own free will; your forgiving me is not dependent on my opinion if you should forgive me or not. For us to reconcile, however, you need to do your part, and I need to do mine. If I do not do my part, we might not reconcile.

For example, if I borrow $5,000 from you, and I do not pay you back, you may decide to let go of my debt and tear up the promissory note, I take no active part in this transaction. You did this of your own free will—you forgave me. However, for us to reconcile, I have a duty, and you have a duty.

Forgiveness is a willful act, not according to capacity.

Forgiveness is a choice, not a capability. You may choose to forgive a person or not. If you are upset with someone right now, you are able to choose at this moment, while you are reading this book, to forgive them, and raise your heart to the Lord saying, "I release the debt of this person, they owe me nothing."

Reconciliation is conditional; however, forgiveness is unconditional.

Forgiveness cannot be conditional; I cannot place conditions for forgiveness to occur. Our Lord forgave all our sins on the cross. On the other hand, reconciliation is conditional. God placed a condition for us to be reconciled with Him: to "put on the new man" (Ephesians 4:24), to live a life of holiness (cf. 1 Peter 1:15), because "what communion has light with darkness?" (2 Corinthians 6:14). We cannot live in darkness and be reconciled with God; I cannot be a child of Belial and want to be a child of God (cf. Deuteronomy 13:13; 1 Samuel 2:12 [KJV]; 2 Corinthians 6:15).

Forgiveness	**Reconciliation**
Tearing up / extinguishing the debt	Reinstating the relationship
Depends on one party	Depends on both parties
A willful act	A willful act
Unconditional	Conditional

APPLYING FORGIVENESS AND RECONCILIATION

Let us apply these points to counseling. For example, if two are in disagreement, and one of them gravely wronged the other, I tell the person who has been hurt, "First of all you must make a decision and a choice to forgive the other person, to release the debt against this person, and walk together along the necessary steps for reconciliation." If we reach a point where the other party wants to reconcile, but refuses to change his aggressive behavior, saying, "If this person wants to reconcile with me, this is my nature, he/she must accept me for who I am. I insult, I get angry," then the church stops and says: "No. We cannot reconcile between you. To reconcile, you need to change." If the person refuses to change, I should not pressure the injured party to reconcile with that person. Otherwise, this person who wrongs others will never change. The person must be isolated, as Saint Paul says, "Put away from yourselves the evil person" (1 Corinthians 5:13), until they change themselves. When the person does improve their behavior, then, as Saint Paul says, "Reaffirm your love to him" (2 Corinthians 2:8).

Remember, one cannot be an opponent and a judge simultaneously. The church must decide, not you. Reconciliation is conditional. The church might tell you to set aside the other party for a while, until they repent and change their behavior, and only thereafter will you be encouraged to deal with this person. This is what Saint Paul said: "Come out from among them" because "what communion has light with darkness." and "what accord [have the children of] Christ with Belial?" (2 Corinthians 6:17, 14, 15). This would not be considered strife; I am willing to reconcile, but I am staying away to deliver a message that the person needs to change their behavior, offer genuine repentance, and then reconciliation will be available. My heart is open for reconciliation, but it has to be on good grounds. Forgiveness is unconditional, but reconciliation is conditional.

FORGIVENESS

Forgiveness is a favor you are doing to yourself, not to the other. If you get upset with me and decide not to forgive me, who then is upset? You! Why? Because you did not forgive me. When you decide to forgive me, who will then be at peace? You! I may not care whether you forgive me or not.

Do you think those who crucified our Lord Jesus Christ cared whether He forgave them or not? They did not care! The Lord Christ forgave them in order for healing to take place. The same goes for you; you need to forgive, because it will help you heal. As such, you are doing yourself a favor, not the other person. Reconciliation, however, relieves you both, and both of you will benefit. When we go back to living in peace, we all benefit.

One might ask, "Is it fair that I should forgive my brother, just like that? He offended me, or as in the above mentioned example, he borrowed $5,000, and should I simply forgo this debt? This is not fair. How can I make such a decision?" Our Lord Jesus Christ answered this question for us: "Then Peter came to Him and said, 'Lord, how often shall my brother sin against me, and I forgive him? Up to seven times?' Jesus said to him, 'I do not say to you, up to seven times, but up to seventy times seven'" (Matthew 18:21–22).

Saint Peter must have said, "Is it possible to forgive my brother 70 × 7 times?" Our Lord went on to explain this to him: "Therefore the kingdom of heaven is like a certain king [Our Lord] who wanted to settle accounts with his servants [us]. And when he had begun to settle accounts, one was brought to him who owed him ten thousand talents" (Matthew 18:23–24).

This parable can only be fully understood when you realize the value of these "ten thousand talents." We all know this parable, but when we look at the monetary value of the numbers, the parable takes on a whole new meaning. One talent equals 6,000 denarii, and one denarius is a laborer's daily wage. You might remember this from the parable of those who were hired about the eleventh hour, where he told him, "Did you not agree with me for a denarius?" (Matthew 20:13), so a daily wage is one denarius.

Let us say that, today, a laborer works eight hours a day for $6 an hour, so $6 \times 8 = \$48$. Let us say $50 a day (for easy math) or about $50 a day. So, a denarius, the daily wage of a laborer, is equal to about $50. Now, if one talent equals 6,000 denarii, then how many dollars is that? $300,000. Now, how much did this servant owe? 10,000 talents. At $300,000 a talent, that brings up the servant's total debt to $3,000,000,000. When this laborer, who makes $50 a day, who makes $1,500 a month, owes 3 billion dollars, how many years would it take to repay? It is impossible! In this parable, our Lord Jesus Christ is trying to tell us that it is impossible for us to repay our debt to Him. There is no salvation through my works, "Neither an angel nor an archangel, neither a patriarch nor a prophet" (Gregorian Liturgy, Reconciliation Prayer) is able to save me. The Holy Bible says, "He was not able to pay" (Matthew 18:25). Of course not, where will he get it! He makes $1,500 a month, how could he afford 3 billion dollars?

The parable continues as follows: "His master commanded that he be sold, with his wife and children and all that he had, and that payment be made" (Matthew 18:25). Indeed, we were sold on account of Adam's sin; Adam and all his descendants were sold to the devil, as we say during the Divine Liturgy, "sold on account of our sins," until we repay the debt. Are we able to repay? No. Then we are destined for eternal damnation.

The Holy Bible goes on to say, "The servant therefore fell down before him, saying, 'Master, have patience with me, and I will pay you all'" (Matthew 18:26). He has no idea what he is saying! How could he repay 3 billion dollars! Where will he get them? How many centuries would it take to repay? "Then the master of that servant was moved with compassion" (Matthew 18:27), as we say in the Midnight Praises, "He was overcome by His compassion." Our Lord Jesus Christ was crucified on the cross through His compassion and love, and released him. He told him, "Here is the promissory note for 3 billion dollars, and I am tearing it up. You are free. I forgive you and I do not need anything from you." The Holy Bible says, "not of works, lest anyone should boast" (Ephesians 2:9).

The parable punctuates, "and forgave him the debt," then continues, "But that servant went out and found one of his fellow servants who owed him a hundred denarii" (Matthew 18:27–28). We said one denarius equals $50, so 100 denarii equal $5,000. If his fellow servant makes the same wage of $1,500 a month, then would he be able to repay him? Yes. "And he laid hands on him and took him by the throat" (Matthew 18:28). Note that when the master wanted to settle accounts, it does not say that he took him by the throat, and yet, this servant took his fellow servant by the throat. Our Lord Jesus Christ wants to tell us that we use aggression [or even violence] in dealing with each other. If my brother offends me, I tend to reprimand him severely, "How could you do this? How dare you have the audacity to say this?" and I go on and on until I make him feel like he is nothing. Although, I commit so many sins against God, and I go and say, "Lord, I have sinned. Forgive me." I go to my confession father and say, "I have sinned against God." He says, "Your sins are forgiven," and reads me the absolution. God forgives me so easily, but before I forgive my brother, I reprimand him, disgrace him, and tear into him—that is, if I do forgive him at all.

The parable continues, "and took him by the throat, saying, 'Pay me what you owe!' So his fellow servant fell down at his feet and begged him, saying, 'Have patience with me, and I will pay you all.' And he would not, but went and threw him into prison till he should pay the debt. So when his fellow servants [the angels who lift our deeds to God] saw what had been done, they were very grieved, and came and told their master all that had been done. Then his master, after he had called him, said to him, 'You wicked servant! I forgave you all that debt [$3 billion] because you begged me. Should you not also have had compassion on your fellow servant, just as I had pity on you?' And his master was angry, and delivered him to the torturers [the devils] until he should pay all that was due to him" (Matthew 18:31–34).

Our Lord Jesus Christ adds a very critical verse, "So My heavenly Father also will do to you if each of you, from his heart, does not forgive his brother his trespasses" (Matthew 18:35). If you think it too much to forgive your brother, remember your own indebtedness to God. Think of the three billion dollars that God forgave you and see if it feels fair to forgive your brother his $5,000. This is why I said forgiveness is unconditional; you cannot put limitations to it. God forgave us all, with all our trespasses. Although we do not deserve it, He forgave us out of His love, "for He was overcome by His compassion" (Monday Theotokia) This is why we must be merciful: "Blessed are the merciful, for they shall obtain mercy" (Matthew 5:7).

RECONCILIATION

What should I do to reconcile? First, if you are a counselor, you cannot make peace between people, while you yourself are not at peace. You cannot give what you do not have. You need to start with yourself.

As you are reading these words, raise your heart to the Lord, and count the number of people with whom you are not reconciled. Ask God to forgive you first, because you must have played a role in this mistake, and to also forgive the other. Right now, make the decision to forgive, because when you forgive you will be healed. As I noted previuosly, this is a decision that depends on you, which you can make right now. You can just say, "I release this debt of $5,000. I am going to God, who is the true Physician."

Second, accept responsibility for your mistake before God, saying, "In this situation, I made these mistakes, which I am admitting before You now. I will admit them before my father of confession, and to the other person."

The third step is for you to go and talk to the other person, "If your brother sins against you, go and tell him his fault" (Matthew 18:15). Go and confront him. When? Today. Immediately after reading this book, because we agreed that you must restore your relationships as soon as possible, and not "give place to the devil" (Ephesians 4:27). Do not wait until tomorrow morning. Tonight, you must reach out to the other person and try to start reconciling. I said reconciliation is a process, which may take time, so you must start tonight.

Conditions for Reconciliation
- Make peace with yourself.
- Accept responsibility for your mistakes.
- Go talk to the other person.
- Do it today.

FIVE RULES FOR SUCCESSFUL CONFRONTATION

When it comes to confrontation, some people object that they do not like to confront others. Often this is the case because we do not know how! How do you confront someone properly? Here are a few rules.

First rule: Your goal is to reconcile, not to reveal the other's mistakes. Many times, when we meet to confront someone regarding an issue, our intention is to show the other person their mistakes, having no intention to truly reconcile. I go to show the person where they fell short, and that is it. This is why it does not work. You must go with a heart open to reconciliation and peace, for "blessed are the peacemakers, for they shall be called sons of God" (Matthew 5:9).

Second rule: Talk about the action itself, not about your interpretation of the action, or your analysis of the other person. Say something like, "When you said such and such, it hurt my feelings. When you became angry with me and said such and such, I felt pain in that situation." Many of us, when we come to confront, begin by saying things like, "Why don't you love me? You do not trust me. You are self-centered. You are an arrogant person." All these expressions are judgmental, wherein I am judging the person. When you begin by saying, "You are an arrogant person," that person will naturally lose his temper, and the confrontation will fail. On the other hand, if you say, "This specific action that you did, it hurt me," the other person may begin to explain the situation. Speak about behavior, not about your interpretation or analysis of the other person.

Third rule: Listen to the other person's point of view completely, because many times, during confrontation, your brain is already thinking of a reply while the other is still speaking. We prepare a rebuttal instead of paying attention to what is being said.

Here is an approach found useful in counseling a husband and wife when they have strife. As a counselor, I ask them to confront each other. The husband confronts his wife, telling her what upsets him. Then, when she begins to answer him, he cuts her off. I ask him to listen to her reply until she finishes. As soon as she is done, he wants to respond, but I ask him, before responding, to repeat what she just said. Often, the husband does not know. Why? Because he was not paying attention to what she was saying; he was thinking of how to reply. As long as he does not listen to the viewpoint of the other, he will never reach a solution. I usually tell him, "Obviously you were not listening to her. Please wait while she repeats what she said, and I want you to tell me what she said." Sometimes we have to repeat this yet again, until I teach him how to be a good listener, to be able to listen and understand what the other wants to say. When you confront, you must be ready to listen, not only enter with the purpose of expressing your anger.

Fourth rule: Take responsibility for your mistakes and admit them. As Saint James says, "Confess your trespasses to one another" (James 5:16). Admit: "I treated you wrongly. I lost my temper with you. I used you in this situation." It can relieve the other to know that you are not simply blaming them, but accepting responsibility for your own mistakes.

Fifth rule: Seek forgiveness, and forgive. Tell the other, "I ask you to forgive me for my mistakes, and I forgive you for all your mistakes." If we carry out confrontation in this correct manner, I expect that a big percentage of our disagreements would be settled.

Five rules of confrontation:
- Go with the intention of reconciling.
- Speak about behaviors, not about your interpretation or analysis of the other person.
- Listen to the other's viewpoint.
- Take responsibility for your mistakes.
- Seek forgiveness, and forgive.

STAGES FOR RECONCILIATION

Certainly not all disagreements will be settled; there is a chance that the other person is hard-hearted and will not accept you, even though you apply the five rules above. For this reason, our Lord Jesus Christ said, "Go and tell him his fault between you and him alone" (Matthew 18:15). This is very important. Many family issues worsen because we involve ten or fifteen people, brothers, cousins, relatives, so the problem becomes more complicated. Do it alone, "If he hears you, you have gained your brother. But if he will not hear" (Matthew 18:15–16), which means there is a possibility he will not hear, what would you do then? Would you say I did all I could? No. The Holy Bible continues: "Take with you one or two more" (Matthew 18:16). Again, not ten, just one or two. What are their qualifications? First, that they are godly, spiritual people. Second, that they have wisdom: "He who wins souls is wise" (Proverbs 11:30). Third, that they are not partial, neither toward you, nor toward the other. Fourth, that they are accepted by both parties, not only by one party.

Four conditions for a conciliator/mediator:
1. Spiritual person
2. Wise
3. Neutral
4. Accepted by both parties

"Take with you one or two more, that 'by the mouth of two or three witnesses every word may be established.' And if he refuses to hear them, tell it to the church" (Matthew 18:16–17). If he refuses to listen to the witnesses, then go to the highest judging authority, the church, who will try to reconcile between you. "But if he refuses even to hear the church, let him be to you like a heathen and a tax collector" (Matthew 18:17). At this point, the Church would tell you, "You did all you can, we cannot ask you to do more. You are permitted to take communion, and to pray, but he is like a heathen and a tax collector." The Church can make a decision regarding him.

Let us explain the phrase "like a heathen and a tax collector" (Matthew 18:17). In the Midnight Praises we say, "For you have chosen the publican, and the adulteress you have saved," so, if this heathen or tax collector comes after 10 years seeking reconciliation, having repented and changed his behavior, then you would accept him. In God's love there is no such thing as "too late!" When the lost son returned, his father accepted him. If you say, "It's too late, I can't accept him now," then you did not forgive him. "Like a heathen and a tax collector" (Matthew 18:17) means you are willing to reconcile, but according to the conditions of reconciliation—if they change their behavior. This is why in the Second Epistle to the Corinthians, when the sinner repented, Saint Paul said to "reaffirm your love to him" (2 Corinthians 2:8). My doors are open; whenever the other person wants to reconcile, they can return. This is why I said that God is not reconciled with everyone, because some of us refuse. But God accepts anyone who returns to Him at any moment, repentant. Take for example, the right hand thief who came to God at the last moment of his life. God reconciled with him, and told him, "Today you will be with Me in Paradise" (Luke 23:43).

Reconciliation Stages:
- One on one
- One or two witnesses
- The Church
- As a heathen and a tax collector

TWO WARNINGS

There are two warnings I want to give you:

The first warning: you might initiate reconciliation today, but you may not feel better instantly. Feeling better, inner healing, takes time. Nevertheless, the good news is that because you have begun the reconciliation process, and you forgave, your healing will come sooner. If you discover the obstacle to your healing, this will speed up the process. So the first warning is that, if you do not feel better immediately, do not despair. On the contrary, this first encounter will accelerate the healing process for you.

The second warning: when you go to talk to the other person, remember that their reaction could be improper. Do not regret it, saying, "Is this what I get for doing what I was told? All I got were a few words I could do without!" Do not regret what you have done.

A father wanted to teach his son about forgiveness and reconciliation. The son constantly complained about his brother. The father told the son, "Each time your brother yells at you, come to me, and I will give you $5." The boy went from being upset with his brother over every altercation, to being happy every time his brother yelled at him, because he knew he would get $5 from his father. What happened? Instead of focusing on his brother's offense, he began to focus on the reward. This is what God told us: "Blessed are you when they revile and persecute you and say all kinds of evil against you falsely for My sake. Rejoice and be exceedingly glad, for great is your reward in heaven" (Matthew 5:11–12). If you try to reconcile, but he rejects you, saying "all kinds of evil against you falsely," rejoice. God just deposited $5 into your heavenly piggy bank! Do not be upset, you have just received your good reward in heaven.

We are children of God, "The children of God ... are manifest" (1 John 3:10), as being peacemakers: "Blessed are the peacemakers, for they shall be called children of God" (Matthew 5:9). You cannot be a counselor, making peace between people, if you yourself are not reconciled with someone. Initiate peace, initiate reconciliation, and may the God of peace grant us His peace, which surpasses all understanding (cf. Philippians 4:7). Amen.

www.ingramcontent.com/pod-product-compliance
Lightning Source LLC
Chambersburg PA
CBHW031309060426
42444CB00032B/828